IN THE BACK SEAT WITH PRINCE CHARMING

Sex, Pregnancy & Healing:
A Teen Mom's Story of Life Turned Upside Down

By: Dee Dee Gooding

Disclaimer: The information and ideas in this book are for educational purposes only and are based upon the author's personal experience, research, and opinion. This book is not intended to be a substitute for consulting with an appropriate health care provider. Any changes or decisions about your medical care should be discussed with your physician. The author and publisher disclaim any liability arising directly or indirectly from this book.

ISBN: 978-0615814711

TABLE OF CONTENTS

INTRODUCTION

———— ❄ ————

*H*ave you ever felt like an outsider? Like you just didn't fit in? Even if it was just for a moment, can you remember how uncomfortable it felt? Or maybe you've felt like an outcast for a long time. Whatever your circumstances may be, most girls, at some point, fear that they aren't fitting in. I certainly had my share of those experiences.

This is a book about belonging, bullying, abuse, popularity, being the new girl, drugs, alcohol, friendships, boyfriends and…sex. You may wonder how all of this fits together, but believe me, it does! And when the pressures of life pile up and no one seems to understand you, it's quite possible you'll be forced to confront the issues. Sometimes, you may deal with your problems constructively, but other times, you may slip and fall. Do things you'll later regret. Engage in risky behaviors. Say words you can never take back. And sometimes, for some of you, you'll find yourself "in the back seat with Prince Charming." And from that experience, you may find yourself pregnant…just like I did.

Now for the big questions: How do you deal with those uncomfortable feelings? What are you willing to do to fit in? What do you do when you feel like you're riding an emotional roller coaster? Do you keep your feelings bottled up inside of you? Do you explode? Do you ever do or say things you later regret?

In this book, you will get an inside look at my story. After learning about my experiences, I think you'll agree that impulsive actions and bad decisions have a way of catching up with you. And many times, the consequences of those choices are permanent. Irreversible. Forever.

MY STORY

———— ❋ ————

"How could this happen to me?"

 D onna warned me. She knew.

On numerous occasions, my older sister had warned me that I should drop my group of friends. Find a better crowd – kids who were more like Matt. Did I listen to her? Of course not.

At this point in time, I was seventeen – almost an adult. My mother had lost all control of me, and Donna treated me more like a daughter than a sister. It was Donna who told me to find better friends, better role models, better values. It was Donna who worried that I was having unprotected sex. It was Donna who suggested that I go to the local clinic for birth control.

I'll never forget that day. We stepped out of the bright sunlight into the cool, air-conditioned offices of the clinic in Santa Rosa, California. Donna insisted that I take a pregnancy test, and the clinic offered free, confidential testing. By going here, my parents would never need to know.

Thank God we went; because that was the day I found out I was pregnant. Not just a little bit pregnant, either, but three months pregnant! When the nurse delivered the shocking news, we both screamed, "Oh, my God!" Donna and I just sat there in the doctor's office, staring at each other. My mind was reeling: *What am I going to do with this pregnancy? Adoption? Abortion?* Then reality set in: *I'm not even with Matt, the child's father! I'm running around with my new boyfriend, Boner, in his old Ford Pinto! What am I doing? Help!*

My sister drove me home from the clinic that day, discussing my "options." But I couldn't think clearly; I just sat in the car and cried, paralyzed with fear. Here I was a junior in high school, where my main concerns were boys, friends, and parties. I wondered what my future was going to be like. My poor choices had led to this disastrous day, and I couldn't believe I had only myself to blame for the careless risks that I had taken on more than one occasion.

As we pulled into the driveway, I tried to imagine breaking the news to my parents, but my mind kept returning to the single question that replayed itself over and over in my head like a bad song on the radio: "How could this happen to me?"

The Early Years in the Moitoza Family

I never expected my life to turn out this way – pregnant and unmarried at age seventeen. Up until that fateful day, my life had been relatively simple. We were a typical middle-class family: two parents, working father, and stay-at-home mom. That secure feeling of having my mother there when I came home from school added a lot of stability to my life. We didn't have much in the way of material possessions, but we seemed to get along just fine with what we did have. During the 70's and 80's not too many women worked, so most kids I knew had a mom at home. Coming from a "normal" home, I thought I was immune to problems that other people had. My parents were married (divorce was never an option in those days), I had an older sister who loved me, and we lived in a nice home. Big problems were for other people, right? Maybe if I had looked closer, I would have realized that everything in my life wasn't as perfect as it seemed.

Our mother, an assertive red-headed Irish woman, took care of the cooking, cleaning, and child rearing. However, I believe that she felt trapped being home all day, and these feelings surfaced as anger towards my sister and me. Sometimes, we thought she was going crazy, for her moods would swing wildly; we could never predict what she would say or do next. She was often nasty to her family at the drop of a hat, and then other times she would give us the silent treatment – especially with my father. Later, we found out that she went through menopause at an early age, and hormones may have played a part in the unpredictable behavior. Unfortunately, as a young child, I had no idea what was happening, and I found it difficult to walk through the land mine of her moods. Though she fulfilled the traditional "duties" of a stay-at-home mother – cooking our meals, cleaning the house, taking care of me and Donna – something told me that Mom would have preferred to be somewhere else in time if it were up to her.

My father was a quiet man, completely different from Mom. An extraordinarily large Portuguese man, Dad worked hard outside of the home, and I admired his work ethic, kindness, and honesty. Back then, most men were motivated to make ends meet for the family, and they did their jobs well. Dad was no exception. Although my father meant well, he left most family responsibilities to Mom, and she seemed to resent his lack of presence in our day-to-day lives.

My sister Donna was two years older, and from my earliest memories, she helped to keep me grounded. She had everything the other girls wanted; she was intelligent, thin, tall, tan, and – to top it all off – had beautiful blonde hair. All the boys liked her, and the girls hated her. I was extremely jealous, especially as a young child. Donna was always the slender one. Me? I had dirty blonde hair and was round as a butterball – you know, like a Thanksgiving turkey! Who knows? It could have been all of the Ding-Dong's and Ho-Ho's (snack foods) we ate back then. Whatever the reason, it wasn't until I turned twelve that I lost the baby fat and became quite skinny. Through all of my insecurities of living in the shadow of Perfect Big Sister Donna, I tried to copy her in every way. I not only dressed like her but also tried to pick up her mannerisms. No matter what I did, I couldn't compete with my ugly braces and scrawny body. Academically, Donna was a straight-A student, while I was lucky to be pulling C's. Over time, I resigned myself to the fact that I would just be "Donna's little sister."

In some ways, it was good that I was forced to establish my own identity, as I was the more athletic one. I competed in track and field events at the age of ten, often coming in first or second place. Though I was proud of myself, it saddened me at times, because I don't recall my parents ever attending my meets. Athletics keep kids focused and instill confidence. Don't all of us yearn for praise and compliments, especially as children? Sometimes I think if my parents had encouraged me with my gift of running, I may have made different choices as I got older.

Besides sports, I was very creative and won several art competitions in middle school. Through these accomplishments, I even made the local paper on several occasions, which boosted my low self-esteem and made me more popular with my classmates.

I was the spunky one in the family, and my philosophy was that rules were made to be broken. If we didn't listen to her, Mom would say, "Wait until your father gets home," but that made no difference to me. For example, as preteens, Donna and I both had braces, complete with humongous headgear. My sister, being the people-pleaser, wore her device. I thought the hideous metal contraption looked as if she could pick up radio signals! But Donna never wanted to disappoint anyone, especially my mother. Instead of being like Donna and listening to Mom, I would do my own thing. As for my own headgear, I refused to wear it and threw that disgusting metal mechanism into the trash! When it came to chores, Donna always did hers – on time, without complaint. Instead of just sucking it up and getting it over with, I bargained with Donna to do my jobs. Of course, this attitude got me into trouble, but I learned that if I did get caught, I could use my sense of humor to get me out of the situations I invariably found myself in.

Through these normal growing pains, it was my mother who had to deal with two pre-teen girls and their antics (especially mine!). I don't think dad knew how to handle his blossoming teen girls, so he left the parenting decisions to Mom. But he did make one crucial decision that changed all of our lives – the decision to move to a new town.

The Move

*D*onna was in high school, and I was in eighth grade. My father received a promotion with the company he worked for at the time, and we would be leaving our hometown of Pinole, California, a large suburb in the Bay area of San Francisco. The new job was located in the small town of Rohnert Park. According to Dad, the promotion was too good to pass up, and he felt this was the best decision for the family. Donna and I hated the idea of moving, but we were never asked. Back then children were supposed to be "seen and not heard". We didn't know anyone in that town! Did my father understand how difficult it is to make new friends in a new school, especially as a teenager in a small town where everyone had known everyone else forever? "Cow Town," we called it, referring to this rural town where we didn't know a soul. I resented my parents for moving us away from our friends and family I had grown up with. I know that Donna felt the same way.

After the move, we had to make new friends and find our place in this small country town. My sister and I quickly found ourselves following very different paths; while Donna chose to live up to our parents' standards by taking the academic route, I chose to do the opposite. I wasn't necessarily a bad kid, but I was curious about people, and I began to hang out with the kids who lived on the edge. You know the type – the ones who were into sex, drugs, and rock music. They were not at all interested in school or listening to their parents. Most of them hung out at the corner convenience store, smoking cigarettes and cutting school. The plus side of having a group of friends like this was that they protected me from the more popular group of girls who I'm sure felt threatened by the new "city girl" who suddenly showed up in their town. See, those popular girls would bully me, afraid I was going to take their boyfriends away from them. I guess my six-inch heels and my designer jeans didn't help matters in this little country town! They just wanted my life to be hell, and they were going to do whatever it took to make me miserable. Hanging out with the "stoners" gave me a sense of security and belonging.

Most of my friends in this rebel group came from single-parent families, so they spent many hours alone while their moms or dads were at work. Within months, my friends had introduced me to smoking pot, which escalated into cocaine use. They also did other addictive drugs like LSD, mushrooms, and prescription pills. I knew it was wrong, so I tried to limit myself by refusing the "hard" drugs. Most of the time, I smoked pot just to fit in, but I never felt like this was really "me." I knew about the dangers of drugs and the benefits of a healthy lifestyle. At times, I would try to teach my friends some of these lessons, but as much as I tried, most of them were headed on a path for destruction. They were used to the party scene; in fact, some of their parents modeled similar addictive behaviors at home. Sadly, addiction took over many of their lives; they didn't seem to know any better. I often ask myself today, *where are they now? Jail? Rehab? On the streets?* Lack of education played a big role in many of my friends' lives. But I knew better, and knowingly rejecting everything my parents taught me made me feel even worse about myself, especially when I knew that Donna would never do drugs or hang out with kids like this.

I remember one particular evening when we were partying after school. My friend Brad almost died from an overdose of prescription pills. Something was horribly wrong when I walked into the bathroom and found him curled up in a ball in the tub. I tried to wake him, but he had taken a pill called yellow jackets and wasn't responding to anything around him. I ran out into the living room. "Something's wrong with Brad! We've got to call his parents!" I cried.

Everyone looked at me with bored expressions. I guess they were too high to care, but all of them said no. "Look," one friend explained, "there's no way we can call his parents! Do you want to get caught?" We put him in a bedroom to sleep it off, and after a couple of hours Brad came to. The guys loaded him into one of their cars and drove him home. I have no idea how his parents reacted, nor did I care. As I said, we were young and thought we were invincible.

This incident *did* scare me enough to look for a new group of friends. I decided I needed to find motivated friends with higher goals and values that matched my family's belief system. It was difficult to find a new clique, though, because as I mentioned, the popular kids were not open to the new girl joining the group. I wasn't playing sports and didn't get good grades, so I had very little in common with this desirable group of students. But I didn't want to be a loner, so I tried my hardest to fit in with kids whose lives seemed to revolve around glamour and fun.

During this difficult time, I couldn't help but consider the "what-ifs": *What if we had stayed back in Pinole? What if I still had my old group of friends?* But our father made the choice to move, and communication in our family was unheard of, especially from the children. "Children are to be seen and not heard," was a popular expression during those years, so I was forced to suffer in silence. Sometimes, I felt like money was more important to Dad than his daughters' own happiness. Even Mom seemed unhappy, but I don't think she said much for fear of offending my father who was so proud of his promotion. She struggled to meet new friends, and I'm sure her failure to cultivate a network of friends was difficult for someone so outgoing. Dad seemed to think we would just pick up where we left off. Of course that wasn't the case, especially for me. It wasn't until I met Matt that life seemed to improve – or so I thought.

Matt

I was now in ninth grade, and Donna introduced me to my first serious boyfriend. Somehow, Donna had learned to fit in with the popular kids, Matt was part of the "in" crowd. He was a good-looking, charming football jock. At 5'11", 160 pounds and with an athletic body, I instantly fell in love. Matt had soft, thick brown hair, and his smile could light up any room. He knew how to look good, and his sweet, shy nature won the hearts of many girls. He also had the best bad-ass car in town – a red Mustang convertible! This was the most popular car at the time, and the girls were jealous that I was the one who got to make out with hot Matt in his cool car.

Matt came from a family like mine, and our similar family values bonded us together. We had fun on our dates, and over time our relationship grew. Whenever I would cut school, Matt would show disappointment in me. He especially didn't like the fact that I still hung onto some of my old, stoner friends. Being older, he would reluctantly buy cigarettes for me and my friends, even though he knew it wasn't a healthy choice for us, which he told me many times. Besides being an athlete, Matt was a great student, too. He was a teacher's aide in my math class, and needless to say, this was the only class I did well in! I found I could charm my teachers (especially the male ones), and my freshman year became a fun, free-spirited time for me. *Why not enjoy myself?* I would think. By then, I realized I had the personality and looks to pull it off.

I enjoyed going to Matt's football games, but many times I would just hang out with my friends and get high instead of really watching my boyfriend play. Matt would often look for me in the stands, and I would give him that cute little wave that would excuse me from my "bad" behavior. Matt would smile, and I knew he was happy that I was there, supporting him. After the game, lots of girls would crowd around him. When that happened, I would immediately take my stance and walk over to let them know Matt was mine. Remember, I had the friends who were ready to fight anybody who crossed them, and these girls knew better than to mess with me! They knew they'd live to regret it if they ever tried to steal Matt from me. Matt and I went to many parties together, and we attended other sporting events, hand in hand. We soon became a high-profile pair, and we liked knowing we were a popular couple. There were times over the next several years when we would drift apart, but eventually we would find ourselves getting back together again; certainly, on-again, off-again relationships are not that uncommon during the high school years.

One Night of Passion

By the time I was seventeen, I thought I was mature enough to take the next step: yes, the "hush" word… SEX! I often thought about birth control, but I was too scared to talk to my mother about this touchy subject. Back then, sex was not talked about with our parents; I think they believed that if they didn't talk about it, then we weren't doing it!

I was definitely the one who pursued Matt at the time. I thought that sex would make me feel even more wanted and loved, which I felt I was not getting from my parents, especially my father. Ever since the move, Dad was spending more time at work and less time with the family. That left me and Donna with Mom, and her style of parenting wasn't the most nurturing.

It was a Saturday night. My parents thought I was sleeping over at one of my girlfriend's houses. They knew I was no angel, but somehow they bought into my lie that evening. Matt and I drove to a place called "Gravity Hill." This was a make out point where all the kids went to party and socialize. That night we were all having fun with our friends, listening to music and drinking. Even Matt had a few beers in him.

Soon it was getting late, and most of our friends had to leave for fear of getting in trouble with their parents. None of us were supposed to be there – like me, most of the kids had made up stories to cover their whereabouts. As car after car drove down the hill, Matt and I found ourselves alone, and my feelings about what was going to happen next overwhelmed me. We were both virgins, and though we had already discussed having sex, I was still scared.

After doing "the deed," I felt embarrassed and self-conscious with Matt. He seemed just as uncomfortable as I was. Despite the awkwardness, we spent the rest of the night in his red Mustang. I really thought we were in love and would be together forever. Holding each other that night was electric, and I eventually relaxed enough to fall asleep in Matt's arms.

The next morning, we were awakened by the sun and thought we'd better head for home before our parents found out where we were. As we drove through the countryside, we were very quiet. I think we both felt somewhat guilty for lying to our parents. When we got home, Matt gave me a soft kiss and told me he would call later. Meanwhile, I was hoping my mother would not ask me any questions about last night ("How was the sleepover? Did you have fun?"). She would instantly know I was lying. I didn't want to hear her crap, either, if she found out. I shuddered to consider the repercussions I would have to suffer if she knew. Like Matt's family, my parents were very strict, and I knew I would be in big trouble if anything leaked out.

After that night of passion, the excitement of dating Matt seemed to disappear from our relationship. Little did we know, but we had been robbed of our innocence at such a young age in more ways than one, and our lives would never be the same. I felt I had done something terribly wrong and wished that I had a mother I could talk to about my feelings. No one taught me about birth control, and sometimes late at night I would panic, worried that I had gotten pregnant from unprotected sex. But by morning, life got in the way of my worries, and I continued through the upcoming months, oblivious to the warning signs that something *had* changed.

After losing my virginity, I was like a ship without a sail, heading in whatever direction attracted my interest at the time, regardless if it were good or bad. Suddenly, I started noticing other guys. My friends were pressuring me to date other boys, so I somewhat reluctantly broke up with

Matt. I'm sure the break-up surprised him; I think he was as in love with me as I had been with him, but I couldn't explain my feelings. After sharing that intimate evening together, something shifted. Maybe I had changed. So many times I would ignore Matt at school. If he called me on the phone, I wouldn't even return his calls. Yes, I was being a bitch, to say the least! In my mind, I felt like other opportunities were passing me by. I didn't even care if I hurt Matt's feelings; I just wanted to have fun again. For some reason, I thought other guys would make me feel beautiful, and I needed that confidence once again.

For a time, the new guys would make me feel special and wanted, just like a fairy tale princess. But when life got tough, I would run back to Matt, and he always had open arms for me. He would do anything for me, and he kept me grounded. When I was with him, he encouraged me to make better choices – stay away from drugs, drinking, and any other unhealthy activities my friends were pressuring me to do. Though I knew how much he cared, I still wanted to be that fun, party girl. Little did I know that through this time, I was carrying Matt's child.

A New Guy

During my on-again, off-again time with Matt, I met another guy at a party. He was four years older, and I found this very exciting. Plus, he showered me with attention, which I loved. I was flattered that he even showed an interest in me because he was *so* drop-dead gorgeous. He was a well-built guy who worked out with weights so that his body was as strong as a brick house. He had brown hair, and dark eyes to match. Unknown to me at the time, he came from a completely dysfunctional family, and his nickname was "Boner." Hello?! With a name like that, this should have been my first clue as to who I was hooking up with. At twenty-one, Boner jumped from job to job, and boy did he liked to party! I didn't care, though; he was a challenge and I had always liked living on the edge. Unaware that I was pregnant, I continued partying with Boner in his "awesome Ford Pinto." What was I thinking?

The first time Boner took me to his house, I stared with disbelief. His family and house were nothing like I'd ever seen before: driving up a gravel road towards the alley where he lived, all I saw were broken-down cars, growling pit bulls in the driveway, and a mother who looked like a truck driver with a cigarette dangling from her mouth. This scene should have been a red flag to me that this wasn't the life I was used to, and to this day I wonder what I ever saw in this guy. But Boner was a good con-artist; he often told me his family was a bunch of dirt bags, but he was nothing like them! That lie should have been clue number two, and I should have run as far away from this situation as humanly possible. My mother always said, "You are a product of how you are raised," and in Boner's case, I would soon find out the hard way that she was right.

We would often party at my friend's house and play pool downstairs. No parents were ever home, nor did they care what we were doing. Everyone would get wasted, and I was always worried. *How I was going to get back home that evening?* Everyone was drunk or high (or both). I knew if I missed my midnight curfew, I would be on restriction for weeks, so I was always the sober one of the group and had more responsibility then any of the losers I was hanging with.

If my parents had known what I was doing, they would have quickly put a stop to it. This was not me, but I could not seem to find a place where I truly fit in. All I could do was bitterly wish we had never moved to this tiny town that was bringing such heartbreak and anxiety into my life. I often wonder what was missing in my life. I grew up believing I never quite fit into any group, and I always found fault with everything I did. I doubted the choices I made, even in the simplest situations. Was it the lack of confidence that was instilled in me at such a young age by a verbally abusive mother? Was it my father, loving but absent through my teenage years?

After a couple of months of hanging out with Boner, my sister suggested I go to the free clinic for a pregnancy test; by the time I told Donna how concerned I was that

I might be pregnant, I had already missed my period for two months – duh! The news that I was, indeed, pregnant, horrified me, and I knew my life would never be the same again. Based on the time frame, I knew the father was Matt, but that was the only thing I felt certain about at the time.

That evening, Donna insisted we sit our parents down to tell them that they'd soon be grandparents. Abortion did cross my mind, but being naïve at the time, I was not aware of my options – remember, I never had an adult to talk to about life's lessons. However, even if abortion was an option, our family could never afford it. So before we broke the news to my parents, I thought, *Great. This doesn't look good for our "All-American family!"*

After a nice dinner prepared by my mother, we decided to break the news. My sister started the conversation, but I couldn't wait any longer. I blurted out, "I'm pregnant!" *Okay, I said it,* I thought. My father gave me "that look," the one filled with disappointment. Before Dad could respond, my mom freaked out. She started shouting, "How did this happen?" and, "Answer me!" I couldn't respond but thought to myself sarcastically, *How do you think this happened, Mom?*

She railed at me, saying things like, "What are the neighbors going to think?" and trying to come up with solutions. I just couldn't take the yelling and the questions, so I ran into my room. She followed me into my bedroom, attacking me with a never-ending list of questions. Then she mentioned Matt, talking about how he needs to "take responsibility." The whole time, my mind was swimming with terrible fears and shame: *What will my future be like? I'm so embarrassed!*

Signs of Abuse

O nce I found out I was pregnant, I dropped out of school, too scared and embarrassed to continue my senior year. No longer with the "in" crowd, the boys suddenly disappeared – except for Boner. I wished someone had warned be about abusive boyfriends back then because this guy spelled disaster. He was a drinker who dabbled in drugs, and he often showed signs of anger management problems. All of these issues gradually poisoned our relationship.

One night I was at the movies with a friend, and upon returning to her house, we discovered Boner in my girlfriend's driveway, waiting for me. I immediately knew trouble was brewing from his folded arms and angry, flashing eyes. I started to feel scared, and my friend's parents weren't home at the time, so it was just us three standing outside. He had been drinking and demanded to know where I had been. I said, "At the movies."

Apparently, he doubted my story, and before I knew what was happening, Boner bashed the windows out of my car. With blood dripping from his clenched fists, I stared at him in shocked horror. My girlfriend yelled to her boyfriend, who was in the house. He ran over to us, prepared to calm Boner down. I stood there frozen, afraid if I got in Boner's way, I may be the one with a fist in my face. Luckily, Boner took a walk to calm down. Still shaking, I got into my car and drove home with bashed-out windows. As freezing air hit my face and glass littered the car seats, I knew one thing: I was screwing up my life and felt utterly disgusted with myself.

I don't know why I continued the relationship with Boner, but I'm sure my lack of confidence played a key role in my poor decision-making – again. Still unaware of the signs of abuse, I caved in when Boner called the next day, begging for my forgiveness. "I'm sorry!" he sobbed, reassuring me that our future would be better if I just worked with him a little. At the time, I didn't know that "working with him" meant doing everything on his terms. He never hit me, yet the emotional abuse was just as bad for my self-esteem. I found myself in a vicious cycle; he insulted me and called me names, but when I got fed up and threatened to leave, he would come back begging. I'd always buy into his pathetic behavior. Over time, his mistreatment got worse, and within a few months Boner thought he owned me. His possessiveness of my every move began taking over my life.

Surprisingly, when Boner found out I was pregnant, he didn't show any kind of reaction. It didn't seem to bother him, which should have been another warning. Instead, he promised he'd help raise this child as his own. This seemed strange, since we had been dating for a short time. I wondered, *What is he thinking? Doesn't it make him angry that I'm pregnant with another man's child?* His dysfunctional behaviors were signs and red flags, but I chose not to read them, or maybe I didn't know how to read them. No one had educated me on the signs of abuse, I never had seen anything like this in my family, and I didn't know how to handle the situation.

The Pregnancy

As the months passed, I grew bigger and bigger. I thought about calling Matt to let him know that I was carrying his child. Part of me feared that he would be just as disgusted with me as I was, and the more I thought about his reaction the more difficult picking up the phone became. Besides, he had a new girlfriend now and was trying to move on with his life. After several agonizing weeks, I finally worked up the nerve to make the call. Fingers trembling, I dialed his number and held my breath. After several rings, I heard his voice on the other end. I couldn't do it. I hung up the phone, paralyzed by fear and shame.

As my pregnancy continued, I sat in my room most of the time, too embarrassed to let anyone see me getting fat at my young age. I had dropped out of high school shortly after learning I was pregnant, so the only time I went out was for my doctor's appointments. I always went by myself, sitting in the waiting room with the older, married women. They would stare at me, and I knew what they were thinking: *That poor, young girl! All by herself, with no one to help her!* At those times, I wished I had Matt or my mother to help me through this difficult situation. But Matt had his girlfriend, and my mother felt it was my responsibility since I got myself into this predicament. I felt like I was on a deserted island, just me and my unborn child. I had no one to talk to, and I had so many questions. But I was too embarrassed and scared to ask anyone. In my mind, there was no turning back.

Eight Months Pregnant

I somehow kept my relationship going with Boner throughout my entire pregnancy. I was so low at this point in my life that I needed someone to fill the void. Boner often poured out his heart to me about his horrible family life, and he always tried to make me feel sorry for him. In the beginning I found his stories tragic, and I did everything in my power to "save" him from his sad life by being his loyal girlfriend. Over time, though, I was beginning to see a different side of him. These stories weren't meant to gain my sympathy; they were meant to manipulate me into staying with him by feeling so guilty about his life that I'd do anything for him. By the time I was eight months into the pregnancy, I felt exhausted all the time, and Boner was zapping me of all my energy. My own fears and Boner's demands overwhelmed me. I started thinking about Matt. *What is the right thing to do?* Matt was such a wonderful person, and I began to wonder why I had ever let him go in the first place. *What the hell is wrong with me?* I asked myself as I compared sweet, responsible Matt to the controlling, pathetic Boner.

Labor Day

I went into labor on December 14, 1981. At the time, I was only eight months pregnant, but I had not taken good care of myself during the pregnancy. Looking back, I believe this lack of care may have prompted the early labor. The delivery process was completely unknown, and no one had offered any advice concerning the agony that I would be in for. It was just me and my sister during this very scary event. Unprepared physically and emotionally, I was completely unaware of the tremendous pain that was awaiting me over the next twenty-four hours! Finally, I delivered an adorable 6 pound, 9 ounce baby boy. I named him Dominic after his great-grandfather. Donna phoned Matt with the news, which was news to me; I had no idea that she had been keeping in touch with him throughout the entire pregnancy. To say I was shocked when Matt arrived at the hospital would be an understatement! Imagine this hospital room scene: Matt, his new girlfriend, Boner and me!

Matt and Boner together in the same room, the tension was unmistakable. Without thinking, I blurted out "Matt, get rid of that girlfriend of yours!" to which he responded, "Only after you lose the drama in your life!" Once Boner realized that *he* was the drama Matt referred to, he argued that the baby was his, though we all knew that was impossible due to the pregnancy timeline.

Finally, I knew what I had to do. "Leave!" I commanded in the sternest voice I could muster. Not sure how he would respond, I was somewhat surprised when he left without another word and only a glare from his eyes. "See ya!" I called to his retreating figure in the doorway. That was the last I saw of Boner. After months of trying to rid myself of this difficult boyfriend, I finally did it! I still don't know how my simple directive worked, but it did. During all of this chaos, my parents and sister were standing in the doorway, listening. They later told me they were wondering if I'd make the right decision by being with Matt, my true love. Imagine their relief when I finally kicked Boner out of my life for good!

Shortly after telling Boner to leave, Matt did the same with his girlfriend (much more gently, of course!). Now it was just the two of us and our new bundle of joy. I had always felt comfortable and content with this man, and his kindhearted ways had won me over. Though he was a man of few words, I knew just by looking at Matt that he hoped we could become a family. I was tired of running around, trying to find my place in the world. So, I turned to Matt once again to fill in the blanks of my life with the hope of a happy family life. I was confident we would marry, and we could give our new baby Dominic the life he deserved.

All through the pregnancy, my parents had urged me to put the baby up for adoption, but I hadn't given it much thought. First of all, I didn't understand the whole adoption process, and I just assumed that I would raise the baby – in my mind, that was the only option. However, my mother wasn't so easily convinced.

Matt had stepped out of the hospital room to give me some time to myself. Moments later, I heard a soft knock on the door. It was my mom and a lady from our church. Without a word, I knew what they wanted – this woman was there to adopt my adorable baby boy! I couldn't believe it: I carried this baby for nine months and there was no way I was going to let someone else take him! I held Dominic in my arms tightly, to show this church lady that I was never letting him go. All I wanted was for my mother and this woman to leave so I could get started with my wonderful life; I would get married, raise Dominic with Matt by my side, and we would all live happily ever after, just like all the fairy tales I loved as a child. I never thought that I might be a single parent, on my own someday, responsible in every way for this child.

My mother looked at me expectantly, so I turned to the woman. "If you're here to discuss my options about adopting my son, you can just take your Bible and go visit some other girls who want to get rid of their children! This baby is mine, and I never intend to give him up!"

Without another word, the woman and my mother left the room, leaving me alone with Dominic and my thoughts.

To this day, my mother has never mentioned that incident, and I sometimes wonder how our lives would have changed if I had considered the option of adoption.

Making Our Way as a Young Family

After returning to my parents' home with Dominic, I found myself ill-prepared to raise an infant. First, I had no furniture or crib since I delivered him a month early. I think that in many ways, I had convinced myself this wasn't really happening – I wasn't really having a baby. I wasn't really going to be a mother. Obviously, the lies I told myself ended with the delivery of Dominic and the harsh reality of being a teenage mom.

Since Dominic was a colicky baby, I didn't get much sleep, nor did anyone else in the house. My mother felt the baby was my responsibility and chose not to help much. Between sleepless nights and lack of emotional support during the day, I began to feel depressed and isolated. I needed a break so badly, and this whole ordeal forced me to think more and more about Matt. As he continued to visit us in the early months, it became clear that we were interested in getting back together. We would try to figure out ways to spend time together as a couple. Certainly, this wasn't my parent's responsibility or his, and my family made sure we knew that we were, more or less, on our own.

Once, when the pressure became too much, I packed up my bundle of joy to visit some of my "old friends." Spending time with them meant that Dominic was exposed to constant smoking and drinking, and within a few weeks, I realized that this life was worse for Dominic than living in my parents' house with no support.

Robbed of my teenage years and confused about my future, I couldn't help but feel sorry for myself as the mounting responsibilities of parenthood started hitting me like a ton of bricks. At eighteen, I was considered an "adult." It was time to act like a grown-up whether I liked it or not. I had always lived in the moment, but I never considered the repercussions of my actions.

After much soul-searching, I decided to build a better life for me and for Dominic by going back to school for my GED. After all these years, I finally had the equivalent of a high school diploma! As I started to make better choices, my parents agreed to babysit for me. With some extra time on my hands, I started taking college courses. Being able to manage going to college and raising Dominic helped to boost my confidence level. I even started setting goals for the future and began feeling pretty good about myself – until my mother stepped in again to disrupt my steady progress. She told me she felt I was taking advantage of her by living at home. According to her, I was "having my fun" while the burden of raising the baby rested on her shoulders.

She said, "It's time to grow up. Take total responsibility for this child of yours!" I was shocked. Did she really think I was living with my parents because I wanted to? I knew I couldn't afford to be on my own, so this arrangement arose from sheer necessity.

Soon, my mother started pressuring me to marry Matt. "You're acting like you're married, anyway, so why not tie the knot?" she asked constantly. Under pressure to "grow up," I decided marriage would be the best decision for everyone – especially for Mom.

My parents called Matt's family to plan the wedding. Both families were excited for Matt and me. One evening, Matt's parents came over for dinner to discuss the big day and to see their grandson for the first time. Though part of me was excited, another part wondered, *Is this how it's supposed to happen?* This wasn't anything like the fairytale books I read as a child. I began to think those books were a lie, feeding gullible children the idea that the prince always sweeps the fair maiden off her feet, and everyone lives happily ever after. *Is Matt my prince?* I had no official proposal...no asking for my hand in marriage...not even a ring! No, this was nothing like my dreams. Instead, my mother orchestrated the event, and as I sat at the table, I couldn't help but think, *This should be a decision between Matt and me.* It was happening so fast – my mother led the conversation, and no one could get a word in edgewise. She wanted the ceremony to happen quickly.

Within five months, I walked down the aisle with two hundred guests looking at us. I made the most of the day, trying to block out everything else and focus on my husband-to-be. We already had a two year old son together, and part of me was embarrassed. I knew this wasn't "acceptable" behavior, and even though I loved Matt, something still felt wrong. However, we enjoyed the reception, and as we danced the night away, I convinced myself that everything was falling into place. *This is my happily ever after...right?*

By the next morning, we were back to business as usual, which meant Matt returned to work while I cared for Dominic. We couldn't afford to take a honeymoon, and our families were in no position to treat us, so we returned to our duties at home. Life continued as it had before.

I took my role as a mother seriously and cherished our family time together. Dominic and I would often go to the beach or the park and play while Matt was working, and I made it a point to read to my son daily. When Matt returned from a long day at the store, he would play with Dominic and then tuck him into bed with a good-night kiss. My family lived within walking distance from our apartment, so we frequently visited them for dinner and game nights. On those nights, my grandmother would make her famous sugar cookies. Grandma gave old-fashioned advice on how to be the best person I could be, and I absorbed her messages like a sponge. She was the one person in my life who always gave me the encouragement and confidence I craved. I could talk to her about the concerns I had about my life as a wife and mother, and her wise words reassured me that everything would be alright. Thanks to my grandmother's loving ways, I felt special, and I will forever be indebted to her for her kind spirit and love.

Married Life

As our marriage progressed, our lack of maturity took its toll on us. We rarely went out as a couple, and most of the time we argued over money and how it was being spent. We couldn't pay the rent and soon were handed our eviction notice. With no place to live, life seemed to be headed down the path I so desperately wanted to avoid. As Matt and I grew apart, I knew I didn't want to settle for this lifestyle. Our marriage was crumbling, and I made the difficult decision to return to my parents' house – without Matt. We tried to continue the relationship for a couple of months, but the separation only led to more arguments. Finally, I decided to end the marriage. This was no surprise to Matt, and we decided to get a divorce.

On my own again, I quickly secured a job at our local Safeway bakery, but I knew this was a job – not a career. As the major breadwinner for me and Dominic, I felt the pressure to create more stability for my tiny family. By following in the footsteps of my beloved grandmother, I went to beauty school full-time while Dominic went to daycare. Like before, my mother softened as I made better choices by taking a more active role in helping me raise Dominic. After graduation from beauty school, I went on several interviews and with great recommendations from my teachers, secured a job as a hair stylist at a local salon. Within a short time, I built a loyal client base, and I enjoyed going to work every day; the close working relationships with coworkers made my work environment exciting. Soon, I had saved enough money to move out on my own. Dominic and I lived simply, yet I felt proud that I could fully support my family for the first time in my life. Matt still came to visit, but I could tell he enjoyed his single life. Although I loved Dominic with all my heart, there were times that I missed the freedom that Matt enjoyed. I often would hear about other friends going to college, dating, partying, and having the time of their lives; hearing this would only make me feel worse, but I was determined to make our family life as fulfilling as possible. At the time, Dominic was six years old and missing his father, yet I didn't realize the impact divorce could have on a child.

Dating Once Again

I started dating again, but most guys didn't seem interested in sticking around when they learned I had a child. I can't tell you how many times dates stood me up, and I felt completely pathetic for involving myself with men like this. After months of getting nowhere, I grew tired of dating losers who could care less about me or my child. What I really wanted was someone down to earth and had compassion for others in the same way I did.

Instead of pursuing the dating scene further, I decided to slow down and just enjoy being a mom. The bar scene was not for me, and I knew this strategy led me to the wrong guys anyway. My sister, who was always looking out for my well-being, wanted nothing more for me than to settle down with a wholesome guy, and she was convinced she knew who that guy was! Donna just happened to work with a man she felt would be a perfect match.

Bruce

My sister gave Bruce my number, and he called me that same evening to arrange our first date. When I saw him for the first time, an image of the tall, gorgeous country singer Toby Keith popped into my mind. With Bruce's baby blue eyes and masculine build, I felt an instant attraction. Over dinner that evening in San Francisco, I found him to be a good listener. We talked about Dominic, and I could tell he was captivated by me, which made me feel special. An added bonus was that Bruce wasn't a drinker like most of the guys his age. He actually preferred family activities over partying at the bars. This amazed me, based on previous boyfriends. Bruce would be a great family man, and I found this part of him to be irresistible.

I wanted to take the relationship slowly, and we spent many evenings playing board games at home instead of partying in a loud, smoke-filled bar. Sometimes Bruce would spend the night in our spare room. I certainly enjoyed having a man in the house, and best of all, Bruce made it clear that he liked me for who I was. He never tried to change me. With all of his strengths, however, there was something about him that I didn't like, though I couldn't put my finger on it. Instead of listening to my intuition, I continued the relationship, relieved to be involved with someone stable and caring.

Bruce filled in all the gaps of my life, especially the times when I felt lonely. He certainly knew how to give me what I needed – compliments to boost my confidence and attentiveness to Dominic and me.

Sometimes, his attention became smothering; he wanted to be with me constantly, and when we were together he would drone on and on about topics of little interest to me. For example, he loved John Deere tractors, which struck me as immature, especially when he dragged me to stores to check them out! I also remember one time when we went to the movies, and Bruce threw candy at the back of people's heads while hiding behind me to make it look like *I* had done it! *Real funny.* These incidents should have clued me in that I didn't really love him. We would have been better off as friends, and I should have stopped looking for a man to complete me. I was doing just fine on my own, and Bruce was clearly not for me.

As the months passed, I realized that sense of challenge was missing from the relationship; Bruce was way too predictable. I should have just followed my gut feelings and run away, but with Bruce always being available, I settled into a romantic relationship with him. Part of me feared that I might be missing out on a great person, so in the end I married him. He was definitely not the type of guy I would usually go for, but I figured, What the hell? I don't even recall how he proposed to me or what the ring looked like. Only a few family members attended this second wedding in Lake Tahoe, and I later found out that Donna and my best friend were taking bets in the back of the chapel as to how long this marriage would last! Like my first wedding, there was no money for a honeymoon, so right after the weekend wedding, it was back to work and the normal family routine.

After being married for a couple of months, I found out I was pregnant. We were both excited, especially Bruce, who had never had a child. This was a dream come true for him! During our marriage, I was the one who made all the decisions for our family and who took care of the finances.

I quickly discovered that Bruce didn't have goals in life like I did. He was content to tinker around the house and let me take care of everything. We lived in a comfortable condominium, and life was going as well as could be expected. Bruce worked as a heavy equipment driver while I worked part-time as a hair dresser. As I grew bigger with our second child it became difficult to work, and I quit my job.

Brandon arrived on June 25, 1991. He was the best baby ever – he never cried and always had smile on his face. This time, my entire family – Mom, Dad, and Donna

– were there to support us at the time of the delivery, and I thought, *This is how life was supposed to be!* I wanted to cherish this time, since I felt that opportunity had passed me by with Dominic's birth. I opened a day care in my home to bring in extra income, and my business quickly grew to caring for five children daily. I didn't make much money, yet I felt like I was contributing in some way. Dominic enjoyed being a big brother, and he liked having all the kids around. He would often help with Brandon while I tended to the household chores.

Unfortunately, Bruce's seasonal job as a truck driver proved to be unpredictable, and the bills started to pile up as money became tight. We could no longer afford the condominium. Being forced to move four times in four years sickened me, so I started thinking that I'd better seek a more secure job, though I resented having to give up my stay-at-home mom status. Reluctantly, I accepted a job at Oroweat Breads at their day-old bakery store. With my personality, looks, and work ethic, I quickly got promoted. In very little time I began managing their Napa store. Bruce continued to stay at home, content to lie on the couch and let me bring in the money. His idea of parenting was watching TV and eating fast food from Burger King. During this time, we argued constantly about how to raise Dominic, who was almost a teenager. Bruce didn't appreciate Dominic's bad attitude, and this took a tremendous toll on our marriage. Dominic already had emotional problems, and the tension with Bruce didn't help.

I didn't need a crystal ball to see where my future was heading. I decided, *Enough's enough!* One evening after I returned from work, tired and overwhelmed, I told this big guy, who now resembled Santa Claus, "Get your stuff, and get the hell out of our lives!" Bruce just sat on the sofa, staring at me. Eventually, he got up and packed his bags (right down to the light bulbs!), and we didn't see him again for six years. No phone calls, no gifts for the children on birthdays or at Christmas. This reassured me that I had made the right decision to leave. We were better off without Bruce in our lives.

I packed what little we had and returned to my parents' house to live – yet another setback in our lives. Bruce moved back with his parents, where he still lives at fifty years of age. Brandon was five and Dominic was fifteen, and though my parents' house was comfortable enough, we still were Crammed into one bedroom.

Moving back home angered my mother. She told me she had enough of my failed relationships and that it was time to think more about my children's lives. She went on to tell me the only reason they took me in was for the sake of the grandchildren. She said, "Dee Dee, it's time to get your life together. Think about your actions and the people you are hurting before you get yourself into a messy relationship again." On a daily basis, she would express her disapproval of me. She had this way of making me feel like I was always doing something wrong. Whenever she would give me yet another disapproving look, I would look at my own kids and feel deep regret for what I had done to them; my poor choices in men were consuming everyone's lives! I tried hard not to impose on my parents by offering to pay for groceries and keeping the house as clean as possible. No matter what I did, it never seemed to be good enough for my mother, so I had to content myself with the knowledge that I was doing the best I could for my children. Unfortunately, my best wasn't enough to help Dominic with his struggles.

Dominic

Dominic's mood swings were becoming more severe by the day. I found myself over-compensating for his depression, wondering if my bad habits while pregnant had contributed to his problems. Before I knew I was pregnant, I still indulged in alcohol, and there were times I hadn't eaten properly for fear of gaining weight. *Had these actions harmed Dominic? Does this explain those inner demons that seem to haunt him?*

As Dominic's behavior worsened, Matt turned a blind eye to his son's issues. Now remarried, Matt had his own family to think about. I constantly blamed myself for my failure to discipline Dominic properly in his early years. Working twelve-hour days left me exhausted, with little time for anything but the basics.

For a brief time, Dominic moved in with Matt, but he quickly decided he didn't like Matt's rules. I received a call one day at work; it was Dominic, begging to move back in with me. He promised he'd improve his grades and behavior, that he was ready to turn his life around. These were the words I longed to hear, and I welcomed him back with open arms. This would be our new start. But just as fairy tales come to an end, my fantasy of a happy little family eroded.

When Dominic entered high school, I encouraged him to continue his education, afraid he would make choices similar to mine. But Dominic always took the difficult path – the one filled with sorrow and heartbreak. Dominic hated school and so did his friends. Later, I learned that he spent more time in our community park than he did at school. I suspected that he was doing drugs, but I never investigated. I was afraid of what I might uncover. Instead, I looked the other way. I couldn't handle any more stress and knew that I wasn't equipped to help my troubled son. I suppose I was being selfish, but I felt overwhelmed, barely hanging onto my own sanity.

At one point, I called a counselor to help Dominic. She diagnosed him with depression and prescribed Prozac, thinking this would solve the problem. Little did I know, but instead of taking the drug, Dominic sold his prescription to make extra money on the streets. He continued challenging me at every turn. I felt frustrated that I couldn't help my child. I thought that he definitely needed a male figure to help straighten him out; obviously he wasn't listening to me. As Dominic's behavior spiraled out of control, he began sneaking out in the middle of the night. God only knows what he did until 2 AM. All I knew was that he would return home drunk or on drugs and sleep through most of the next day. I lived in constant fear for his life.

But life with Dominic was not all bad. He was a handsome young man with dark hair and beautiful dark eyes. In his early years, he proved himself to be an impeccable writer with an incredible imagination, and he rarely asked for help with homework. I can't help but wonder what his life would have been like if he pursued his talents and stayed in school.

Today

Sadly, Dominic has chosen a self-destructive path. At the age of thirty, Dominic chooses drugs over everything else. Like me, he became a teenage father, but his wife has since left him to protect their children. I can hardly blame her. His behavior has forced him in many emergency rooms throughout the years, and today, his house is his car. My son has chosen drugs and getting his next fix over family and friends. Dominic's backpack is his only friend now. In that backpack is everything he owns. He has lost it all.

After divorcing Bruce, I ended up meeting Tony, my current husband. Together, we gave birth to a beautiful son,

Dylan, who is now thirteen. We live in beautiful Lake Tahoe, California, and Tony has been the hands-on father my two other sons never had.

Meanwhile, my second son, twenty-one-year-old Brandon, is pursuing his dream of becoming a fire fighter. Though his life is not without problems, it appears that my ability to parent him later in life served him well. Maybe being a teen mom doesn't explain away all of Dominic's problems, but I know in my heart that my inability to raise him the way I would have wanted definitely contributed to the problems he faces today.

Reflections

As a young girl, you may have grown up with fairy tales like Cinderella, Sleeping Beauty, and Snow White. Many of these tales promote the idea that a handsome, rich man will ride into your life and take care of you forever – that your "prince" will make you feel beautiful and special in every way. Isn't this what many girls want? I certainly did! I looked for that prince and even got up on that fairy tale horse more than once, but I fell off many times along the way.

Instead of working on myself and my own self-confidence, I chose to spend most of my time trying to attract the "Fairy Tale Prince." This led me to search for a man who doesn't exist. Three husbands later, I came to the conclusion that fairy tales are not real, and I wish I had been told this at a young age. That's why I'm telling you, if you are looking for your "prince," please understand that this "Cinderella Syndrome" will not make you happy. *You* are the only person who can make yourself truly happy, confident, and fulfilled. This doesn't mean that you can't have a terrific relationship with a guy; it just means that you shouldn't look to another person to make up for what may be missing in your own life.

I encourage you *not* to follow in my footsteps. If I had to do it all over again, I know I would have made different choices. Though I feel I have come full-circle in my life, finally cobbling the pieces back together and forging ahead with a life of "normalcy," the consequences of my actions have created incredible pain and heartache for me and my family. My hope is that after reading my story, you'll take a good, hard look at your own life. Take important decisions seriously, because making the wrong choices can bring consequences into your life you really don't want. Educate yourself, work on being the best you can be, and ultimately make informed decisions that will benefit everyone in your life. I don't wish for anyone to endure the trials and tribulations I did, and if sharing my story prevents heartache for someone else, then I know my struggle was not in vain.

In the rest of this book, I will offers some strategies for preventing teenage pregnancy, the factors leading up to risk-taking behaviors, and a list of *resources* to provide you with further information on this topic. If you feel you don't have anyone to talk to about your problems and feelings, please refer to the Resources section: if I had known about the people and organizations that exist to help people like me, I may not have made some of the decisions I did in my young life.

> "It is not easy to find happiness in ourselves,
> and impossible to find it elsewhere."
> -Agnes Repplier

WHY DO TEENS GET PREGNANT?

————— ✳ —————

Now that you've read my story, let's talk a bit more about why teens get pregnant in the first place. Of course, every situation is unique, each person has personal reasons for his or her behavior, but in my experience and through my research several common themes emerge. Let's take a look at each one and explore some tips to avoid potential dangers and risky behavior:

• Low Self-Esteem / The Desire to be Loved

Self-esteem – mine was extremely low. With a mentally abusive mother I was made to feel not "good enough" at a very early age. No matter what I did or said my mother found fault with it, and this constant barrage of negativity led to feelings of worthlessness. In response, I found myself constantly seeking approval and reinforcement. I wanted somebody – anybody! – to affirm that I was a good person, for I secretly did not believe this about myself. I think that girls today need to learn, in their earliest years, that they need to have confidence in themselves. Some girls may be fortunate enough to have a network of caring, loving adults who provide a strong foundation for self-confidence. Unfortunately, many girls do not have this advantage. In my opinion, confidence is the key, and whatever a person can do (in a healthy way!) to develop a strong sense of self is crucial for success in all aspects of life.

TIP: A person with a healthy level of self-esteem is one who is comfortable in her own skin. Love yourself for who you are, even when you make mistakes and experience setbacks. Valuing yourself and taking responsibility for the choices you make are essential in order to lead a happy, productive life. Have the confidence to stand up for yourself! Respect yourself (especially your body), and say no to people and activities that will hinder you from growing. Be proud of who you are, and make choices that reflect this pride, even if it means going against the crowd at times. Confident people attract positive people, which lead to fulfilling relationships and friendships.

• Lack of birth control

Ninety percent of teenagers who do not reliably use some form of contraception get pregnant within a year. Those are the cold, hard facts. As a teenager, I thought I was invincible. "Nothing will ever happen to me," I thought. I certainly didn't foresee the consequences from my one night of passion. Let my experience reinforce the fact that, yes, you can get pregnant the first time you have sex. It happens; it happened to me. And remember, even if pregnancy doesn't result, unprotected sex leaves you vulnerable to contracting numerous STD's (sexually-transmitted diseases), such as herpes, genital warts, and HIV. Some of these diseases are untreatable, meaning that you will be stuck with your condition for the rest of your life.

TIP: If you are going to have sex (this includes oral, anal, and vaginal sex), use protection! Don't allow yourself to be pressured into unprotected sex, not even "just once." As you can see from my story, "just once" was enough for me to get pregnant. See the section on How to Prevent Teen Pregnancy in the First Place for more detailed information on birth control.

• Forced Intercourse

Forced intercourse, otherwise known as rape, is a real danger to young women today. Almost 20% of women aged 18-24 have been forced to have sex at least once *(Trends: Child Fact Sheet)* It doesn't matter if the other person is a friend, acquaintance, boyfriend, or stranger – anyone who has sex with you without your consent is engaging in forced intercourse. When this happens with boyfriends many girls blame themselves for "leading him on" or saying no "at the last minute." Remember: you are entitled to say "no" at any time, and if the other person continues to force himself on you it is *not* your fault; even if you are in the middle of sexual activities and decide to stop, the other person should respect your decision. Realize that threats are a form of force too (for example, someone threatens to break up with you or hurt you in order to make you have sex).

TIP: Be safe. If you are on a date or at a party arrive and leave with friends. Be sure that other people know where you are and keep in touch to let others know your whereabouts. Don't go off alone with someone you don't know well. Drinking and drugs may be used to put you in a position where you can't fight back or make good decisions; be aware of the dangers of alcohol and drug use. With male friends and boyfriends, listen to your intuition (your "gut"); for instance I was given many red flags about Boner not being a positive person in my life, but I ignored the warning signs. Luckily, he did not force intercourse on me, but I _did_ suffer in other ways from that relationship. If you listen to that tiny voice that warns you about people who spell "trouble," you can't go wrong – your gut instincts are usually accurate.

• Thinking Life will be Better Somehow

I kept waiting for my Prince Charming – someone to sweep me off my feet, build me up, and make me feel special. Obviously, my life not only got worse, but the men I chose to involve myself with complicated my life. When I was pregnant I thought a baby would love me and make me feel better; however, this is not a healthy reason for having a baby, and I was not prepared for the responsibility that comes with being a mother at such a young age.

TIP: You are in charge of your destiny, including how you feel about yourself. The people you surround yourself with can support you and treat you well, but in the end _you_ are the one to decide how you feel about yourself. That includes your circumstances in life; if you want your life to be better then you need to take action to make that happen! Another person, no matter how much they love you, cannot do that for you. Once you realize that you have the power to make your life magnificent you won't feel the need to find a man or boyfriend to fill in the lonely spaces in your life or make your life better somehow. When you rely on yourself you'll be in the perfect position to meet someone for the right reasons! Remember: _A confident woman will always attract a confident man._

• The Cycle of Teen Pregnancy

If your mother and grandmother were teen moms, your chances are much higher of becoming a teen parent; this is a pattern many of us follow. I was a teen mom, and my son Dominic, became a teen father, too. Like me, I knew my son was not in any position to raise a child. Being a parent is the most difficult job in the world, and now my son is cheating his child out of the benefits of a stable, secure family life.

TIP: If you have not been raised with the best role models in your life, you need to work even harder to break the vicious cycle of dysfunctional behaviors. For example, if you were raised in a single-parent home, have parents who dabbled in drugs and alcohol, you need to stay far away from anyone or anything that reinforces these negative behaviors and patterns. Though I came from a two-parent home with no drug or alcohol problems, the lack of emotional support from my family wreaked havoc on my life; instead of finding love at home, I looked for it in dysfunctional people, situations, and relationships. Be aware of dysfunction in your home, and instead of blaming others for your misfortune, use that awareness to avoid making the same mistakes that others around you have made.

• Teen Moms in the Media

As young girls, we often idolize celebrities due to how famous and beautiful they are. We will copy their behavior, and sometimes we become discontent with who we are. A couple of examples of high-profile teen moms can be seen on MTV's *Sixteen and Pregnant* and *MOM 2*. If you look at these girls' lives off-screen, they are very different from what you see on the show. Many times, they are not with the fathers of their children and they are struggling to pay their bills. Statistics show that most of these girls live at home with their parents, as I did, and they fall below the poverty level. Many of them are likely to drop out of high school and remain single. Jamie Lee Spears and Bristol Palin have displayed themselves publically as teen moms. One plays a very popular teen on a Nickelodeon show, and the other was relatively unknown outside of Alaska until her mother, Sarah Palin, ran for Vice President. Both girls have two things in common: (1) they will both have babies before they graduate high school; and (2) both girls are no longer with the fathers of their children.

TIP: Realize that just because these teen moms are celebrities their lives are not different from ours in some fundamental ways; they still have to shoulder the responsibility of caring for their children, and it is not easy to continue with their education or careers unless they have full-time help. Just like in scripted shows and movies, reality TV is not completely "real."

The Facts

*According to the Centers for Disease
Control and Prevention...*

- The highest teen pregnancy/childbirth rates are found among the socially disadvantaged.

- Of high school students who have had sexual intercourse, 46% of them are currently at risk for contracting HIV (human immunodeficiency virus), other STD's (sexually-transmitted diseases), or becoming pregnant.

Teenpregnancy.org cites the following statistics...

- The United States has the highest teen pregnancy rate in the industrial world (750,000 pregnancies annually), with one third of girls becoming pregnant before the age of 20.

> "Respect yourself enough to walk away from anything that no longer serves you, grows you or makes you happy."
>
> -Robert Tew

BECOMING A TEEN PARENT WILL CHANGE YOUR LIFE... FOREVER!

———— ✳ ————

*T*hink about it. If you become pregnant, your life will be forever changed. First, you now have a child to care for during the next eighteen-plus years, which is a huge commitment in itself. But every other aspect of your life will change too. Consider the drastic differences that will occur in your life in the following areas:

• School

I dropped out of school during my senior year, and though I did go to a continuation school for my GED I always hated school. I felt like it just wasn't for me, and I thought I could just raise my son and work. Now that I look back, that was a poor decision. There are so many options to assist pregnant young women who wish to continue their education *and* raise a child. Many colleges provide free child care right on campus; the mothers can take their children with them while they are in school thus getting an education while knowing that their children are well-cared for! For someone who wants to keep the baby and finish her education this alternative could work well. Check your local community colleges and four-year institutions for more information.

- **Work**

  Many times, teen moms drop out of high school to find work to support their children. The chances of find a well-paying job dwindle as a drop-out; without a high school diploma or college degree, you're work options are very limited, and unless you have extraordinary financial support from another source you will find yourself challenged with money issues. In addition, you may be limited to jobs with (1) little chance for advancement, or (2) long, inconvenient hours that force you to leave your child alone (or without quality supervision).

- **Friends**

  Friendships were never the same for me after I became pregnant. I lost most of my friends; no one wanted to hang out with me, and I couldn't take part in "normal" teenage activities with them anymore. Even if your friends support you throughout your pregnancy it is important to realize that no matter what you will always have an extra level of responsibility that they will not be able to relate to. You will always need to consider the needs of your family first, and you will miss out on many of the fun, carefree activities that are a typical part of the teen years because you now need to be more responsible and act like an adult.

> "Be that strong girl that everyone knew would make it through the worst, be that fearless girl, the one who would dare to do anything, be that independent girl who didn't need a man, be that girl who never backed down."
>
> -Taylor Swift

HOW TO PREVENT TEEN PREGNANCY IN THE FIRST PLACE...

———— ❋ ————

O n the following pages, I will discuss the different ways teen pregnancy can be prevented. Depending on your values, religious beliefs, and personal opinions, certain options will probably resonate more closely with you than others. All of the suggestions below, though, will go a long way in preventing teen pregnancy and all of the difficulties being pregnant as a young girl entails.

• Abstinence: The Benefits of Waiting

Of course, if you abstain from having sex you will be certain to avoid pregnancy. People make the decision to abstain from sex for different reasons. If you have a strong religious background you have probably been advised to wait to have sex until you are married. For those of you who have been brought up with these values you may decide to follow this advice; if that is the case, you can feel confident knowing that you are following your church's (or personal) moral code. Other girls choose to wait so they do not have to worry about the risks associated with engaging in sexual relationships.

As I have mentioned, pregnancy is not the only possible consequence; STD's are a very real concern too. Another reason you may consider waiting is to avoid getting a "reputation"; girls and boys alike may view you differently if they know that you are sexually active, and you may regret those choices especially if you develop a "bad reputation." The emotional benefit of waiting is worth considering as well. That is, when you wait, you will still have that excitement, that anticipation of your "first time." When you give in to having sex at an early age, however, all of that is gone. I believe that when you wait, in the long run, you will find your Prince Charming. I truly believe that. Many other guys will perceive you as a young women worthy of respect – believe me, it's true! Finally, if you abstain from sex, you will be able to devote your time to other worthwhile pursuits, such as schoolwork, sports, other extra-curricular activities, and meaningful time with friends and family.

• Contraception
Birth control is often a controversial issue between teens, parents, schools, religious groups, etc. Teaching

about birth control is often misunderstood and thought to be a signal to teens and young adults that it's "okay" to have sex. The idea that young people may somehow "go wild" if protected from getting pregnant by using birth control is oftentimes not the case. However, it is true that many teens that get pregnant have a steady boyfriend and practice monogamy. Even one night of passion, perhaps at the senior prom or elsewhere, can result in an unwanted pregnancy.

If you decide to use birth control (the Pill, condom, etc.) be sure to look at the resources at the end of this book for more details. Talk to a doctor to get the facts about birth control; though well-meaning, friends don't always have their facts straight, and they may give you faulty information that you may later regret. Find an adult you can talk to as this he or she can assist you in making important decisions. A trusted adult you can confide in will also provide you with much-needed support as well. Read the next section on *Emotional Support* for more details on this topic.

MY ADVICE TO YOU...

I'd like to encourage you *not* to have sex outside of marriage, but if you do choose to be sexually active (or you think it "may" happen), I strongly encourage you to explore all options available for birth control. Information and education is crucial in order to make the right birth control decision for you. Make a choice that best suits your lifestyle and pocketbook. I have said this before, but I can't stress enough the importance of talking to someone about this topic. If you don't have someone in your family to confide in, you may choose to speak to a counselor at your local branch of Planned Parenthood. The counselors at Planned Parenthood can answer your questions and help you make decisions about birth control. Or, maybe you know of a trustworthy, knowledgeable adult at your school (coach, teacher, guidance counselor) who can guide you. Please take the time to read, talk to others, and think about your options before making a final decision. You want to feel good about your choices and behavior, and taking your time when it comes to something as important as having sex is a must.

> "As we grow up, we realize it is less important to have lots of friends, and more important to have real ones."
>
> -Unknown

TIPS FOR LEADING A HEALTHY LIFESTYLE

---*---

- **Recognize Abuse (Physical, Verbal, and Emotional)**

    Many times, emotional and verbal abuse is difficult to detect; you may not have any physical signs of abuse, so people overlook this as abuse, and it's difficult for anyone to prove. I have been in abusive situation many times, and I can tell you the signs to look for. If you are spending time with someone who is controlling your everyday life, or if this person has to know where you are at all times, this is a red flag. If your partner displays emotions by regularly yelling at you, this is not normal, acceptable behavior. In these instances you need to leave the situation as soon as possible. Here are some more examples of emotional abuse from Lundy Bandcraft's book, *Why Does He Do That?*

    1. He is controlling.

2. He is possessive.

3. Nothing is his fault.

4. He is self-centered; it's his way and no other way.

5. He abuses drugs or alcohol.

6. He pressures you for sex.

7. He gets serious too quickly about the relationship.

8. He intimidates you when he's angry.

9. He has negative attitudes toward girls.

10. He treats you differently around others people.

11. He appears to be attracted to drama in his life.

Abusive relationships spell disaster for the victims; if you are involved in this type of relationship please make a plan and then get out of the situation as soon as you safely can. If you can rid yourself of abusive people you will be able to say goodbye to a lifetime of dysfunction.

• Know When to Leave a Relationship

Even if the relationship hasn't reached an abusive level there are times when you are better off on your own. Read my Top 12 Signs for "When It's Time to Move On" below. Be honest with yourself and decide if your current relationship is healthy or harmful:

1. You live in the past moments more than the present (all of your good memories with this person happened in the past).

2. The relationship brings you more pain than joy.

3. The other person expects you to change for him/her.

4. You stay in an unhealthy relationship, thinking that the other person will change, or that you can change your partner.

5. You justify your partner's actions to yourself and others, but you know in your heart that the other person's behavior is harmful to you, dangerous to others, and/or wrong.

6. This person hurts you physically, emotionally, or verbally. (Note: this one falls in the abuse category. See the advice above, and prepare to get out of the relationship!)

7. You have tried to address problems in the relationship, but the problems reoccur over and over, no matter how much you or the other person has agreed to change.

8. You and your partner have values and beliefs that are drastically different.

9. The relationship is holding you back; the relationship prevents you from growing as an individual, and you feel stifled, smothered, or "trapped."

10. You partner checks up on you constantly, calling or texting you nonstop.

11. When you do something that makes you proud of yourself, s/he puts you down.

12. Your partner talks about you, your friends, and/or family inappropriately or disrespectfully.

- **Find Positive Role Models (The Importance of Strong Values)**

I have studied many families throughout my adult life and read case studies in my college classes. I have found that it does not matter if you're rich, poor, or middle class; it's more important for a family to have strong values and structure in order to raise healthy children with a positive self-concept. Having fun together, laughing and loving unconditionally – these are examples of ways to build a strong foundation for happy, healthy children (and later adults). Friction in the family and parents who do not stay together can lead to uncertainty for a child. Alcohol and drug abuse in a family system will make problems even worse. In these difficult situations, a child might feel abandoned and less confident, which may lead the child down a road of self-destruction.

But what if you don't have a strong family system? What if you come from a broken home or a dysfunctional atmosphere? In this instance it is crucial that you build a support network with people (inside or outside of your family) who can be role models, a positive influence on you, and who will listen to you when you need them. Look for friends, clergy, teachers, mentors – even other friends' parents! – who may be able to guide you during difficult times. Many schools and towns have mentor/ mentee programs or big brother/big sister organizations; look into these options so that you never feel alone. Surround yourself with positive people who will help you to be your personal best. Be sure your support network includes older people too; even if you feel as if they can't relate to everything in your life. Older people possess knowledge about the world that your friends may not have. Their wise words can assist you as you navigate the obstacles on the path to growing up. Ask yourself these questions when deciding if a person is supportive of you:

- Is this person encouraging most of the time?

- Does s/he want what's best for you? (Note: This doesn't mean that you always get what you want. People who care for you want you to be safe and will look out for you in this way.)

- Is this person honest with you? Will s/he tell you the truth, even if it's not what you want to hear?

- Are you comfortable talking to this person and asking questions?

- Do you trust this person? Is s/he reliable; can you count on him or her?

- Is this person positive – a good role model for you to follow?

- If you answered "yes" to most of these questions, this person is someone who will most definitely guide you in the right direction through your teen years (and beyond!).

WHAT TO DO IF YOU ARE PREGNANT?

———— ❈ ————

What if you *are* pregnant? If you find yourself in this situation, it is time to be honest with yourself. Allow yourself to experience the mixed emotions that may surface during this uncertain time. You may feel sad, angry, anxious, confused, or all of the above. This is normal, and you need to give yourself time to work through these emotions. But don't go through this time alone like I did; find someone to talk to, whether it's a parent, other family member, doctor, counselor, teacher, etc. The important thing is to find someone you are comfortable with – someone you can talk to without fear of judgment and criticism.

Perhaps you have several people who can be part of your support network. You'll need to find someone who welcomes your questions, allows you to vent your frustrations, and really listens to you. You will want someone who is there for you to discuss your options regarding the pregnancy. Find someone who will go to doctor's appointments with you, and if you are considering adoption or abortion, someone who can accompany you to these appointments. Many times when you are feeling emotional it is difficult to fully comprehend messages from doctors and other professionals while discussing your options. Having another person there to hear the words and help you work through the decision-making process gives you a much better chance of making sound decisions that you will feel good about in the upcoming years.

Options to Consider...

The most obvious choice is to deliver the baby and raise him or her yourself. This is certainly a viable option, but be sure that you have fully considered the life changes that you will face as a teen mom. If the child's father is still part of your life, and this option may be an enticing one, but in making your decision think about how you would feel about raising the baby if he were not in the picture. Would you still want to raise your child alone if you found yourself in that situation? I don't mean to be pessimistic, but you need to acknowledge that there are no guarantees in life. You *could* at some point be responsible for this child on your own. Would you still make the same decision or would you change your mind? Once you decide on a course of action regardless of the father's involvement (or lack thereof) you can feel confident that you have considered all aspects of the situation and therefore you are giving your child the best possible start in life that you can offer. Ask yourself, *am I prepared, mentally, emotionally, physically, and financially for this responsibility?* If you decide that yes, you plan to keep the baby, please take parenting classes. Read books. Talk to other mothers – look into joining a mother's group.

All of these actions will help you learn how to be the best mother you can be.

Some of you may be considering abortion. If this is an option for you research organizations like Planned Parenthood, The National Abortion Federation, and The World Health Organization for information and locations of clinics. Many of these organizations can connect you with doctors and counselors before making such an important decision. And since abortion is such a controversial issue, you may wish to research "pro-life" and "pro-choice" web sites and organizations. It is imperative that you fully consider the benefits, risks, and moral issues regarding this topic so that you can feel comfortable with whatever decision you make.

Adoption is another option for young women today. During the 1960's and 1970's, if a young girl got pregnant she was often sent off to live with a family member for the nine months of pregnancy. After she delivered the baby a loving family would adopt the child. The young girl would then resume her life – go to college, marry someday, and hopefully reach her life's goals. This arrangement seemed to work for most parties and it was an especially good arrangement for the baby. The young mother, however, would often be the most bothered by this because she would always wonder about her child's well-being.

In the 1980's, the tides changed. Many pregnant teens either aborted the unwanted pregnancy or kept the baby. This has had a devastating effect, as one-third of these girls opted to have abortions. As for the group who decided to carry their babies to term and raise them were at a great risk of committing themselves and their young children to lives of poverty. With 80% of teen mothers living below the poverty line their offspring would many times follow suit.

Clearly, I did not want to consider adoption at the time – I had brought the pregnancy to term, and I wasn't about to give my son up to a stranger! Those were my feelings at the time, and if you are pregnant you may have similar thoughts. In hindsight though, I think that adoption could have been a terrific idea. There are so many people in the world that can't have children and would love to have a baby. For instance, my cousin adopted a child because she couldn't have kids, and she and her husband couldn't be happier.

In addition to giving a priceless gift to another person, the birth mother can get paid a lot of money for giving a child up for adoption. Even if you give your child up for adoption, you can sometimes negotiate an arrangement where you get to visit your child so you can put your mind at ease that s/he is being cared for by loving people. If I had to do it all over again, I would have seriously considered adoption. I simply did not have the maturity level or parenting tools at the time, and I believe that someone else who really was prepared for the awesome responsibility of parenting could have provided a more stable upbringing than I did. See the Resources section for more information regarding adoption.

QUESTIONS TO ASK YOURSELF

———— ✳ ————

*J*ournaling is a great way to get your thoughts on paper where you can see them and gain some clarity about your feelings. Whether you are pregnant, not pregnant, or just reading this book for information, please take some time to fill in the answers to the questions below. Thinking about your values and opinions will help you become more aware of yourself as a person. With greater self-awareness, you are in a better position to make decisions that come from a place of knowing who you are. You are less likely to allow others' opinions to influence you, especially if someone else is pressuring you to take part in something you don't agree with.

Knowing yourself better will also aid you in situations where there should be "red flags." For example, if you know that you try to please everyone around you and you meet someone who is very demanding, you may be aware that this person has a lot of influence over you because you realize that you're bending over backwards to please him. You may even be compromising your values to please another person, but once you realize what you are doing, you have a greater chance of changing your behavior and moving in a positive direction.

JOURNALING

———— ❋ ————

Are You Seeking Prince Charming?

1. What do you think about "Cinderella Syndrome? Have you grown up with the belief that you need to wait for Prince Charming to make everything alright?

2. What are your goals in a relationship? Are you looking for a guy to take care of you? If so, why?

3. Does a handsome, popular, or powerful guy make you feel fulfilled and confident?

4. Do you feel you are worthy of a man who has it all? Why?

5. What do you feel you have to offer in a relationship?

6. What kinds of guys are you attracted to? How healthy are these types of men for you?

7. What do you think about fairy tales and how they apply to your life?

8. Look inside yourself, and list your positives attributes. Think about the compliments you receive for ideas.

Do Now: Look at number 8. These are your strengths, so start working with them! Do anything you can to reach your goals. Prevent yourself from developing the Cinderella complex. Remember, a confident woman is very attractive to the right kind of man.

What Do You Want To Be?

1. What path are you on in life? Have you been making good choices?

2. Do you have a special person in your life who you strive to be like? What is it about this person that you admire?

3. Is there someone in your life who can help you set goals regularly?

4. What do you have to offer people? What are your strengths that set you apart from others?

5. What are your goals in life? Where do you see yourself in ten years?

6. What career do you wish to pursue? What education or training do you need to achieve your goals? Who

can help you along the way (family, friends, guidance counselors, etc.)?

7. If you don't like something about yourself, what can you do to change it?

8. What can you do to let the true you shine?

Do Now: Begin building your support network. Find mentors, people to confide in, and surround yourself with people who build you up. Write down your goals and make a plan for achieving them. Believe in someone or something that gives you strength, like God or a power larger than yourself. It is also helpful to find an adult you admire, and then ask that person questions. This is how you learn and grow.

Your Relationship With Money

1. What are your beliefs about money? Do material possessions define who you are?

2. What can you live without? Do you think you won't be popular unless you have the latest and greatest gadgets or all the designer clothes, shoes, bags, etc.?

3. Do "things" really make us stand out from the crowd?

4. If money were no object, what would you do?

Do Now: Think of creative ideas that you can do to make money. For example, dog walking services, babysitting, and cupcake designing can be a big business! These are just some ideas of things you can do from your home with very little money. As you plan for your future, it is important to find your passion. I've always told my sons and the teen girls I've mentored to consider owning a business someday. Whether it is opening a salon, designing clothes, or starting another kind of business…just do it!

Thinking About Pregnancy

1. Has a boy pressured you into making any decisions you did not like? Do you have an adult you can talk to about this?

2. If you are currently in a sexual relationship, are you on birth control? If not, why not?

3. Have you ever thought about what you would do if you were pregnant? Would you choose to raise the child, or adopt him/her out to a loving family? How do you think your child's life would be, if you chose to raise him/her on your own?

4. If you were pregnant, would you have the financial resources and education to raise your child the way s/he deserves to be raised? Ask yourself the following: Do I have a decent car? A place to live? Money to pay for food, diapers, daycare, etc.?

5. Would you be prepared to be up all night long, feeding and attending to a baby's every need?

6. Would you be prepared for others' judgments about you that come with having a child as a teen? Typically, people will treat you differently.

CONCLUDING THOUGHTS

———— ✳ ————

I care deeply about the choices each and every one of you makes. It is my hope that you have learned through my mistakes. I don't want you to take the same risks, and though I'm not a professional counselor or physiatrist; I am, quite simply, a woman who has "walked the walk" that most helping professionals have not. From raising three sons, ages 30, 21, and 13, I *do* know a thing or two about teens and their struggles.

As a mentor for high-risk teenage girls in our local continuation school, I assist them in changing the way they think about themselves. Confidence-building and working on them to improve their skills will help these young ladies to succeed in the game of life. I am currently taking classes at my local community college, learning how to become a counselor for adolescents with drug and alcohol addictions. Yes, I am doing all of this at the age of 49, but by working my way to an Associate's Degree, I will build a better life for myself!

Your goal in life is to be happy. You have the power to choose who you want to be, so be the greatest and the best that you can possibly be, because in the end, it is *your* journey!.

Enjoy your journey!

Dee Dee

Connect with Dee Dee at
www.princecharmingbook.com

RESOURCES

———— ✻ ————

For excellent information on pregnancy, birth control, abortion, and even relation-ships and body image:
http://www.plannedparenthood.org/

Sponsored by MTV, this site offers information on everything from birth control to options about adoption and abortion:
http://stayteen.org/

For information about teen pregnancy, and tips for parents and guardians:
http://www.cdc.gov/teenpregnancy/

To learn more facts about pregnancy, STD's and birth control, open the pdf file at:
http://www.childrenscolorado.org/pdf/teenage_sex.pdf

For more answers to some frequently asked questions about adoption, visit Adopthelp.com, at:
http://www.adopthelp.com/pregnant/birthmother-faqs.html

This site will help you explore your options regarding abortion and explain the medical procedures:
https://www.prochoice.org/pregnant/options/abortion.html

The World Health Organization explores ways to ensure safe abortions (along with other issues related to abortion):
http://www.who.int/reproductivehealth/publications/unsafe_abortion/en/

CPSIA information can be obtained
at www.ICGtesting.com
Printed in the USA
LVOW01s2306210217
525015LV00007B/183/P